BOOKS BY OGDEN NASH

HARD LINES (1931)
FREE WHEELING (1931)
HAPPY DAYS (1933)
FOUR PROMINENT SO AND SO'S
(1934)
THE PRIMROSE PATH (1935)
THE BAD PARENTS' GARDEN OF
VERSE (1936)
I'M A STRANGER HERE MYSELF
(1938)
GOOD INTENTIONS (1942)

VERSUS (1949)
THE PRIVATE DINING ROOM (1953)
YOU CAN'T GET THERE FROM HERE
(1957)
EVERYONE BUT THEE AND ME (1962)
SANTA GO HOME: A CASE HISTORY
FOR PARENTS (1967)
THERE'S ALWAYS ANOTHER
WINDMILL (1968)
THE OLD DOG BARKS BACKWARDS
(1972)

COLLECTED AND SELECTED

THE FACE IS FAMILIAR (1940)
MANY LONG YEARS AGO (1945)
FAMILY REUNION (1950)
VERSES FROM 1929 ON (1959)
MARRIAGE LINES: NOTES OF A
STUDENT HUSBAND (1964)
BED RIDDANCE: A POSY FOR THE
INDISPOSED (1970)

AVE OGDEN: NASH IN LATIN
(TRANSLATED BY JAMES C.
GLEESON AND BRIAN N. MEYER)
(1973)
I WOULDN'T HAVE MISSED IT:
SELECTED POEMS OF OGDEN NASH
(1975)
A PENNY SAVED IS IMPOSSIBLE (1981)

FOR CHILDREN

THE CRICKET OF CARADOR (WITH
JOSEPH ALGER) (1925)
MUSICAL ZOO (WITH TUNES BY
VERNON DUKE) (1947)
PARENTS KEEP OUT: ELDERLY POEMS
FOR YOUNGERLY READERS (1951)
THE CHRISTMAS THAT ALMOST
WASN'T (1957)
CUSTARD THE DRAGON (1959)
A BOY IS A BOY: THE FUN OF BEING
A BOY (1960)
CUSTARD THE DRAGON AND THE
WICKED KNIGHT (1961)

THE NEW NUTCRACKER SUITE AND
OTHER INNOCENT VERSES (1962)
GIRLS ARE SILLY (1962)
A BOY AND HIS ROOM (1963)
THE ADVENTURES OF ISABEL (1963)
THE UNTOLD ADVENTURES OF
SANTA CLAUS (1964)
THE ANIMAL GARDEN (1965)
THE CRUISE OF THE AARDVARK
(1967)
THE MYSTERIOUS OUPHE (1967)
THE SCROOBIOUS RIP (BY EDWARD
LEAR: COMPLETED BY OGDEN
NASH) (1968)
CUSTARD AND COMPANY 1980

FOR THE THEATER

ONE TOUCH OF VENUS (WITH S. J. PERELMAN) (1944)

EDITED BY OGDEN NASH

NOTHING BUT WODEHOUSE (1932)
THE MOON IS SHINING BRIGHT AS
DAY: AN ANTHOLOGY OF GOOD-
HUMORED VERSE (1953)

I COULDN'T HELP LAUGHING:
STORIES SELECTED AND
INTRODUCED 1957
EVERYBODY OUGHT TO KNOW:
VERSES SELECTED AND
INTRODUCED (1961)

EVERYONE BUT
THEE AND ME

OGDEN NASH

EVERYONE BUT
THEE AND ME

Illustrated by JOHN ALCORN

Little, Brown and Company   •   Boston   •   Toronto

FIRST PAPERBACK EDITION

Library of Congress Cataloging in Publication Data

Nash, Ogden, 1902–1971.
  Everyone but thee and me.

  1. Humorous poetry, American. I. Title.
PS3527.A637E85 1985   811'.52   85-60
ISBN 0-316-59856-9

VB

Published simultaneously in Canada
by Little, Brown & Company (Canada) Limited

PRINTED IN THE UNITED STATES OF AMERICA

Some of these verses have appeared in the following magazines: *The New Yorker, Holiday, Ladies' Home Journal, Harper's, Saturday Review, Sports Illustrated, The Saturday Evening Post, House and Garden, Family Weekly, Suburbia Today,* and *Think*. The author is grateful to David McKay Company, Inc., for permission to reprint a revised version of the introduction to their fabulous art gallery, *Viva Vamp!*

CONTENTS

THE BOOK OF JOB

THE UNSEEING EYE:
THE TRAVEL DIARY OF A NON-OBSERVER

TABLE TALK

[xii]

[xiii]

THE BOOK OF PROVERBS

THE BOOK OF JOB

[2]

UNFORTUNATELY, IT'S
THE ONLY GAME IN TOWN

Often I think that this shoddy world would be more nifty
If all the ostensibly fifty-fifty propositions in it were truly
    fifty-fifty.
How unfortunate that the odds
Are rigged by the gods.
I do not wish to be impious,
But I have observed that all human hazards that mathe-
    matics would declare to be fifty-fifty are actually at
    least fifty-one–forty-nine in favor of Mount Olym-
    pius.
In solitaire, you face the choice of which of two black
    queens to put on a red king; the chance of choosing
    right is an even one, not a long one,
Yet three times out of four you choose the wrong one.
You emerge from a side street onto an avenue, with the
    choice of turning either right or left to reach a given
    address.
Do you walk the wrong way? Yes.
My outraged sense of fair play it would salve
If just once I could pull the right curtain cord the first
    time, or guess which end of the radiator lid conceals
    the valve.
Why when choosing between two lanes leading to a
    highway tollhouse do I take the one containing a
    lady who first hands the collector a twenty-dollar bill
    and next drops her change on the ground?

[3]

Why when quitting a taxi do I invariably down the door
handle when it should be upped and up it when it
should be downed?

By the cosmic shell game I am spellbound.

There is no escape; I am like an oyster, shellbound.

Yes, surely the gods operate according to the fiercest ex-
hortation W. C. Fields ever spake:

Never give a sucker an even break.

HOW CAN ECHO ANSWER
WHAT ECHO CANNOT HEAR?

Why shouldn't I laud my love?
My love is highly laudable;
Indeed, she would be perfection
Were she only always audible.

Why shouldn't I laud her voice,
The welcomest sound I know,
Her voice, which is ever soft?
It is likewise gentle and low —

An excellent thing in woman
And the Wilson's thrush, or veery —
But there are maddening moments
When I wish I had wed a Valkyrie.

Whenever her talk is restricted
To topics inconsequential
She utters it face to face,
With clarity reverential.

Then why, when there's something important to say,
Does she always say it going away?

She'll remark, as she mounts the stairs to bed,
"Oh, some F.B.I. man called and said . . ."
Then her words, like birds too swift for banding,
Vanish with her upon the landing.
"Don't you think we ought . . ." Then she's gone, whereat
The conclusion fades out like the Cheshire Cat.
Yes, her words when weighty with joy or dread
Seem to emerge from the back of her head;
The dénouement supreme, the point of the joke,
Is forever drifting away like smoke.
Knowing her custom, knowing the wont of her,
I spend my life circling to get in front of her.

I'll bet that the poet Herrick,
With Corinna gone a-Maying,
Had to run like a rabbit
To catch what she was saying.

I SUPPOSE THE GREEKS
HAD A COMMERCIAL FOR IT

OR, HAIL, SOLON! HOW'S THY COLON?

At times I fear that my normal nostalgia is transcending
the norm,
That it is becoming nostomania, which I am told is
nostalgia in excessive form.
On the other hand, as into my psychoses I probe,
I conclude that I may not be a nostomaniac, I may simply
be an enteronophobe;
I may simply resent the destiny
Which my submission to TV has made my living room
so intestiny.
In my youth, when instead of dialing ME 7-1212 for
the time of day you just asked it of a wonderful
woman named Central,

Nobody under ninety publicly discussed the condition of
 their entrail.
In the '20's, about which there has perhaps been too much
 tall talk,
I feel there was something to be said for our small talk.
At the risk of appearing to be a gout-ridden old meanie,
I claim that Bufferin's "Out of the stomach and into the
 bloodstream" is a phrase inferior to Mr. Woollcott's
 "Out of these wet clothes and into a dry Martini."
Well, to make a long colon short, while the little ones
 watch their favorite after-dinner show, I bandage
 my eyes with my napkin and dream that I am
 week-ending with Lillian Russell at Lake Placid,
And the genial announcer announces to me that my napkin could be eaten through by two teaspoonfuls of
 concentrated stomach acid.
It was obviously the television, or gastro-enteric, age that
 was foreseen thirty years ago by Doctor Traprock,
 clairvoyant, clear voiced, no Delphic stammerer,
When he penned his prophetic epic, *Through the Ali-
 mentary Canal with Gun and Camera.*

ALIAS AND MELISANDE

OR, GAMMON ME ONCE, GAMMON ME TWICE, YOU CAN COUNT ON GAMMONING ME THRICE

Melisande Misty is a British writer whose detective
stories I greatly admire,

And the latest from her pen I am quick to beg, borrow,
or hire.

She is both ingenious and prolific, in addition to which
she is ethical, or at least I guess so;

Her publishers, however, are simply ingenious, and I
wish that they were less so.

I read a magazine serial of hers entitled *The Case of the
Gruesome Bird*,

And relished it, word by word.

Later, thinking I had encountered a new Misty, I un-
wittingly purchased the English book version under
the original title, *The Paw Incarnadine*,

And this time I just relished it line by line.

Relish gave way to surfeit when I was misled by the new
title of the American hard-cover edition.

I soon recognized *The Case of the Gruesome Bird* and
The Paw Incarnadine, even though they now mas-
queraded as *Too Late the Physician*.

Facing a journey, I purchased an unfamiliar paper-bound
   Misty, despite its lurid name,
And if you think that *Curtains for a Lustful Virgin*
   turned out to be *The Case of the Gruesome Bird* and
   The Paw Incarnadine and *Too Late the Physician,* I
   can only bow my stupid head in shame.
Publishers may squabble among themselves, but on one
   truth they all agree:
A rose by any other name can be sold over and over and
   over, especially to me.

COME, COME, KEROUAC!
MY GENERATION IS
BEATER THAN YOURS

My dictionary defines progress as an advance toward
perfection.

There has been lots of progress during my lifetime, but
I'm afraid it's been heading in the wrong direction.

What is the progress that I see?

The headwaiter has progressed to being a maître-d.;

The airwaves have advanced backward like so many
squids,

And the radio jokes about Bing's horses have become the
TV jokes about Bing's kids.

We have progressed from a baseball czar to a football
czar, and I suppose we'll eventually have a huntin'
and a shootin' and a swimmin' czar,

And now the designers of automobile seats tell us that
men's hip spreads have progressed to being broader
than women's are.

Oriental menaces have not let progress pass them by,

And we have advanced from Fu-Manchu to Chou En-lai.

Once, you just put "The Two Black Crows" on the talk-
ing machine and wound the handle and it played,
but now science has stacked the deck,

And if you want to hear one Little Golden Record you
must be a graduate of Cal. Tech or M.I.T. (which is
sometimes known as No-Cal. Tech).

Progress may have been all right once, but it went on too
      long;
I think progress began to retrogress when Wilbur and
      Orville started tinkering around in Dayton and at
      Kitty Hawk, because I believe that two Wrights
      made a wrong.

VIVA VAMP, VALE VAMP

Oh for the days when vamps were vamps,
Not just a bevy of bulbous scamps.
The vintage vamp was serpentine,
Was madder music and stronger wine.
She ate her bedazzled victims whole,
Body and bank account and soul;
Yet, to lure a bishop from his crosier
She needed no pectoral exposure,
But trapped the prelate passing by
With her melting mouth and harem eye.
A gob of lipstick and mascara
Was weapon enough for Theda Bara;
Pola Negri and Lya de Putti
And sister vampires, when on duty,
Carnivorous night-blooming lilies,
They flaunted neither falsies nor realies.

Oh, whither have the vampires drifted?
All are endowed, but few are gifted.
Tape measures now select the talent
To stimulate the loutish gallant
Who has wits enough, but only just,
To stamp and whistle at a bust.
O modern vamp, I quit my seat,
Throw down my cards and call you cheat;
You could not take a trick, in fact,
Unless the deck were brazenly stacked.

THE BACK OF MINE HAND
TO MINE HOST

Once there was a pawnbroker who got stuck with a batch
of unredeemed slots for used razor blades, and he
said, "Well,
I guess I've got the beginnings of a hotel.
So far as I am aware of,
All I need now is no hooks and some dummy taps marked
'Ice Water,' and the bathrooms are taken care of."
He also didn't need any bureaus — just those combina-
tion desk and dressing tables that your knees won't
fit under, so you can neither write nor primp, and
they have another feature equally fell:
You have to leave your shirts in your suitcase, because
the two lower drawers are filled with blankets and
the top one with telegraph forms and picture post-
cards of the hotel.
He got a mad inventor to invent a bedside lamp with a
three-way switch, so that when you finish your
paperback thriller, either American or Britannian,
Why, you can't turn out your light without turning on
that of your slumbering companion.
He employed one maid for bedmaking and fifty maids
who excel at the sole duty he assigned them,
Which is to wait until you are in a state of extreme disha-
bille and then burst into your room and cry "Just
checking!" and vanish in a puff of smoke, leaving a
smell of sulphur behind them.

[15]

I would recommend this hotel to you if you have a lot
    of old razor blades you have been meaning to get rid
    of because you can't afford to have them gold plated
    or silverized,
Particularly if you regard the cardboard bosoms with
    which your same-day laundered shirts are stuffed
    as an adequate substitute for the buttons which have
    been pulverized.

THE SPOON RAN AWAY
WITH THE DISH?

The ideal TV commercial pins the attention of the viewer,
And I am suffering from one that has pinned my wander-
ing thoughts like shish kebab on a skewer.
Did I ever prick up my ears
When the other night a smiling announcer presented
what he called the most revolutionary dishwashing
discovery in twelve years!
I readily agree that the new discovery is great;
What pinned my attention was trying to remember what
revolutionized dishwashing in 1948.
I was in the most frustrating of the countless predica-
ments I have been among,
Because the answer wasn't even on the tip of my tongue.
I could remember that in 1948 the Cleveland Indians
took the World Series, four games to two, from the
Boston Braves, and Citation won the Derby;
Also that 1948 marked the publication of *The Golden
Hawk,* by Frank Yerby.
Frank Yerby did not win the Nobel award for literature
that year, but T. S. Eliot did — may he long on life
have lease —
And there was no Nobel award for peace.
I recalled clearly that the Pulitzer Prize went to *Tales of
the South Pacific,* by James Michener,
But that was literary stuff — I was groping for something
pantrier, something kitchener.

For that twelve-year-old dishwashing discovery my mind
    continues sleeplessly to grope.
Could it have been the discovery of dish towels? Of
    paper plates? Of hot water? Of soap?
Of course, there was my wife's welcome discovery that
    without my assistance it took her only half the time
    to get the dishes spotless and arid,
But that was in 1931, shortly after we were married.
Anyhow, that's the way my brain has been eroded,
Worrying about a once-revolutionary method of dish-
    washing that has now been outmoded.

STICKS AND STONES MAY BREAK MY BONES, BUT NAMES WILL BREAK MY HEART

I realize that today nothing is more vestigial
Than the highly touted dignity of the individual,
Yet I am touchy about what people call me; about what
    people call me I make much ado.
There are even occasions when I object to being addressed
    as "you."
Such occasions occur in that sob-brother piece on the
    sports page that sets you down in the heart of the
    fray;
It begins, "You are nineteen years old, a raw kid from
    Broken Toe, Ark., and ninety thousand screaming
    maniacs are waiting for you to decide whether to
    play it safe and punt or try to go all the way."
Another journalistic appellation that I give the bird to
Is the one by which as John Q. Public I am referred to.
This term is too repulsive even for the philosophical cigar-
    smoking skipper of the average Manhattan hack;
He calls me Jack.
I am perforce reconciled to policemen calling me Pop
    where once they called me Buster,

[19]

But there is one point at which I take my stand with
    Leonidas and Custer:
Like the sensitive writer Hearn, who emigrated to Japan
    simply because his parents kept calling him Lafcadio,
I plan to quit my native shore the next time some duck-
    headed yahoo calls me Daddy-O.

A POTTED WATCH
NEVER BOILS

OR, MAYBE THAT'S WHAT THEY'VE
BEEN TRYING TO PROVE

You blow yourself to a handsome watch,
The finest, a Swiss, not Dutch or Scotch.
You carry it for a month or so
And realize that it's running slow.
It's no federal case, even one for the mayor,
So you take it back to the watch purveyor.
You state your trouble in terms laconical,
He frowns and screws on his arcane monocle.
To the frown he adds an important pucker
As he opens your watch like an oyster shucker.
He smiles. There is little to be adjusted;
The works are dusty, they need to be dusted.
Six weeks later a postcard informal
Says call for your watch, its pulse is normal.
It's thirty dollars for repairs,
But as long as your watch keeps time, who cares?
You carry it for a month or so
And realize that it's running slow.
What to do? You're only a layman,
So you take it now to a different shaman.
Six weeks and thirty dollars later,
Your watch is still the same cunctator.

You become the oddest of anthologists —
Instead of verse, you collect horologists.
My conclusion about them, I here record it:
They do not repair your watch, they board it.

FURTHER CONCLUSION

There's never anything wrong with your watch,
Swiss or Swahili, Dutch or Scotch,
That money and time and an expert magician
Will not leave in the same condition.

JACK DO-GOOD-FOR-NOTHING

A CURSORY NURSERY TALE
FOR TOT-BAITERS

Once there was a kindhearted lad named Jack Do-Good-
for-Nothing, the only son of a poor widow whom
creditors did importune,

So he set out in the world to make his fortune.

His mother's blessing and a crust of bread was his only
stake,

And pretty soon he saw a frog that was about to be
devoured by a snake.

And he rescued the frog and drove the snake away,

And the frog vowed gratitude to its dying day,

And a little later on in his walk,

Why, he saw a little red hen about to be carried off
by a hawk,

And he rescued the little red hen and drove the hawk
away,

And the little red hen vowed that whenever he was in
trouble his kindness she would repay,

And he walked a few more country blocks,

And he saw a bunny rabbit about to be gobbled up by
a fox,

And he rescued the bunny rabbit before the fox could
    fall on it,
And the bunny rabbit thanked Jack and told him any time
    he needed help, just to call on it,

And after all this rescuing, Jack was huffing and puffing,
And a little farther on the snake and the hawk and the
    fox jumped him, and out of him they beat the stuffing;

They even stole his crust of bread and each ate a third
of it,
And the frog and the little red hen and the bunny rabbit
said they were very sorry when they heard of it.
You see, Jack against a cardinal rule of conduct had been
a transgressor:
Never befriend the oppressed unless you are prepared to
take on the oppressor.

WHOSE BABY? —
A BRIEF INTRODUCTION
TO GRANDPARENTS

You are truly a kindly person, your misanthropy is mostly
a sleeping volcano, like Mauna Loa,
But one thing that awakens it is other people's children,
than which you rate no flora or fauna lower,
So you have spent much of your life cultivating tact and
forebearance

And the art of avoiding other people's children without
    offending their parents,
And just when your allergy to other people's children is
    recognized by those of your friends who seem out to
    emulate the old woman who lived in a shoe,
Why, along come your grandchildren, who are certainly
    other people's children if you grant that your own
    children are people, which some broadminded parents
    do,
And as sure as the filbert is named after St. Philibert and is
    a cultivated variety of hazel,
Your attitude towards other people's children undergoes a
    swift reappraisal.
You ask yourself, trying to be detached and distant,
If instead of rejecting these little strangers you idolized
    them, are you being inconsistent?
No indeed, you sensibly conclude that these particular
    little strangers are the exception to the rule,
Because even when they are mewling and regurgitating in
    their nurse's arms it's a beguiling regurgitation and a
    melodious mewl.
You are in a euphoric humor,
You are tempted to dismiss their parents as mere middle-
    men, necessary only to deliver the finished product
    to the ultimate consumer,
So you mistrust not only their parents but their pedia-
    trician, you become a chronic worrier,

And of their favor you become a shameless currier.

You want fire engines and ambulances kept off the street and the entire work of the household to cease during their slumbers,

And you engage in expensive undeclared competition for their affection with their other grandparents, your opposite numbers.

Eventually you try to adjust your conduct to the greatest handicap a grandparent endures,

The fact that they are other people's, not yours,

So you say to yourself, Hands off, and you promise yourself that the most heartless treatment of them will leave you silent as the grave,

And then you find yourself defending them against their parents next time they misbehave.

There is a proverb often quoted by young Married Couples in China, both Nationalist and Indo-:

When grandparents enter door, discipline fly out window.

THE SENDING OF THE PENS

Ball point pens, ball point pens,
Everywhere I turn, it's ball point pens.

They line the rug from door to door
Like acorns on a forest floor,
They're on the sofa, on the chair,
Under foot and in my hair,
Forming patterns picturesque
On my bureau, on my desk,
Insolently making free
Where my pencils used to be,
And, when gentle evening comes,
In my bed like cracker crumbs.

Ball point pens, ball point pens,
Oh, the visitation of the ball point pens.

Some are sowed like rye or oats
By my wife, who on them dotes,
Some I know are left behind
By parting guests of absent mind,
Some tout investment analyzers
And banks and other advertisers,

But powers mightier than men's
Have joined the game of ball point pens.
Miraculously pens appear
Out of nowhere into here.
Like the gold on Danaë
Ball point pens have showered on me.
They're like the ruthless locust horde
That chastened Egypt for the Lord,
Or like the fabled fall of frogs,
So rain these plastic polliwogs.
Mayhap some sorcerer's apprentice,
Above himself, *non compos mentis,*
Forgetting the magic words, Say when,
Has loosed the raging ball point pen.
One drop of water from a ditch
Breeds millions of bacteria which
Increase to billions neath the lens;
That's how our house breeds ball point pens.

Ball point pens, ball point pens,
One a penny, two a penny, ball point pens,
Who'll buy, who'll buy my ball point pens,
Who'll buy my ball point pens?

NO CONFORMITY
TO ENORMITY!

OR, THE BIGGER THEY ARE,
THE HARDER I FALL

It has been regularly reported by every reporter
'That cars are getting longer and parking spaces are
    getting shorter.
Our curbs are double-lined with automobiles snugger than
    bugs in a rug,

The result of the obvious fact that you can't get five quarts
    into a one-gallon jug.
Yes, the traffic situation has reached a pretty dim pass,
But I wish to speak of a similar and equally frustrating
    impasse.
For this impasse, I know to what we owe our thanks:
We owe them to collusion between the Post Office De-
    partment and the banks.
For example, the Mercantile Seamen's Safe Deposit &
    Trust Company merges with the Patent Attorneys
    & Corn Chandlers Guaranty Company of Lower
    Manhattan, and does the idea of an abbreviated title
    occur to them?
No, the new institution becomes (the initials are my own
    short cut) the M.S.S.D. & T. Co.-P.A. & C.C.G. Co.
    of L.M.
A person who can take one envelope and get that all in —
Well, they could engrave *War and Peace* on the head of
    a pin.
But that's only half an impasse, so the Post Office De-
    partment rushes into the breach;
Whenever two banks merge, it chooses that moment to
    issue a new batch of stamps honoring Johnny Apple-
    seed or National Brush Our Teeth Week, all of
    which are the size of a postcard from Miami Beach,
So now part of the address runs over onto the desk pad,
    but it doesn't really matter, because the part on the
    envelope is covered by the stamp.
But I have no intention of contracting writer's cramp:

I now reply to all reproachful letters from my bank in
    an envelope with no stamps and no address,
And if anybody wants to know who to deliver it to, just
    let them guess.

YOU'VE GOT TO BE
MR. PICKWICK IF YOU WANT
TO ENJOY A PICNIC

Perhaps it's just that I'm lazy,
But I think anybody over six who says "Let's have a picnic" is crazy.
For some years now I have been grown up,
And I get no pleasure out of a warm martini served
in a paper cup.
Picnics consist almost entirely of paper, not only paper
cups, but paper spoons, paper plates, paper napkins,
waxed paper, and the asbestos newspaper that you
try to start the fire with,
Paper that you and I dispose of after our picnics, but
everybody else litters up the county, state, or shire
with.

[36]

There is the Odyssey picnic with no planned picnic site, and this one it is better to be caught dead than alive in,

Because after miles of not being able to choose between bosky dell and shady river bank you end up by eating your picnic in the car in the parking lot of an abandoned drive-in.

There is the inland picnic where you start to tickle and discover that every tickle is a tick,

And the beach picnic where the host didn't realize that the tide would come in so quick.

I always say there is only one kind of picnic where it docsn't matter if you have forgotten the salt and the bottle-opener, and the kids want to go to the bathroom, and the thunder clouds swell and billow like funeral drapery,

And that is where the meal is cooked in the kitchen and served on the dining room table, which is covered with snowy un-papery napery.

[38]

PAVANE FOR A DEAD DOLL

OR, THE PAIN IN
GRANDFATHER'S NECK

I seldom worry about the fate of Java or Sumatra,
But I often worry about the fate of the protagonist of a
　　song once popularized by The Inkspots, or maybe
　　it was Frank Sinatra.
The past of this swooning swain is not difficult to surmise;
He is complaining bitterly about the unsportsmanlike
　　conduct of a group of flirty flirty guys who have upset
　　his love-apple cart with their flirty flirty eyes.
His anguished longing for a doll that other fellows cannot
　　steal would melt a heart of stone,
And he vows that he is goin' to buy a doll that nobody
　　can steal; viz., a paper doll that he can call his own.
He obviously intends to sequestrate this reasonable fac-
　　simile of a chick in some cozy hideaway where its
　　jealous owner can indolently gloat and loll.
An ingenious notion; I simply ask where he's goin' to buy
　　his paper doll.
I pluck this question from my vows-hard-to-swallow file,
Not as a spoil-sport, but simply because in a quarter
　　century of searching I haven't been able to find a
　　paper doll that would satisfy a five-year-old, much
　　less a starry-eyed paper dollophile.

In my youth little girls, whether on a branch line or the
　　Main Line,
When they wanted paper dolls they had a world to choose
　　from, including the fascinating Letty Lane line.
They ranged from pretty to pretty-pretty, they might have
　　been designed by Sir Lawrence Alma-Tadema
Or some other distinguished member of the Royal Acad-
　　ema;
Now, whether in bathing suits or ball gowns or uniforms
　　or civvies,
They look as if they were designed by the people who
　　put out ash trays in the likeness of privies.
Not only are they a far remove from the beaux-arts,
Many of them are plywood, they are not even paper, just
　　their clothes are.
They are mostly part of some forgotten motion picture pro-
　　motion campaign, so if they aren't Shirley or Scarlett
They are named for some once-promising starlet.
I have hunted from hither to yon with a dedication grand-
　　fatherly and solemn,
And I have yet to find a paper doll that is not as vulgar
　　as a café society column.
I have become reluctantly reconciled to buying more
　　expensive gewgaws and folderoldrums;
Today's toy shops are in the paper doldrums.

IS THERE AN OCULIST
IN THE HOUSE?

How often I would that I were one of those homely
    philosophical old codgers
Like, say, Mr. Dooley or Will Rogers,
Because I could then homelily call people's attention to
    the fact that we didn't see eye to eye with the
    Italians so we had a war with them, after which,
    to put it succinkly,

We and the Italians became as close as Goodson and
  Todman or Huntley and Brinkley,
And we didn't see eye to eye with the Germans and we
  had to either fight or bootlick,
So we fought, and now everything between us and the
  Germans is *gemütlich,*
And the Japanese didn't see eye to eye with us, so they
  fought us the soonest,
And today we and the Japanese are of companions the
  boonest.
Now at the daily boasts of "My retaliation can lick your
  retaliation" I am with apprehension stricken,
As one who watches two adolescent hot-rodders careening
  headlong toward each other, each determined to die
  rather than chicken.
Once again there is someone we don't see eye to eye with,
  and maybe I couldn't be dafter,
But I keep wondering if this time we couldn't settle our
  differences before a war instead of after.

AS I WAS SAYING TO ST. PAUL JUST THE OTHER DAY

Opsimathy, says my dictionary, opsimathy is learning
    acquired late;
Opsimathy, I may add, is what is eventually served to
    those who only stand and wait.
I deduce that St. Paul was no stranger to opsimathy.
Take his first epistle to Timothy;
His wits were functioning, though his bones were brittle,
And he wrote, "Bodily exercise profiteth little."
I, too, possess opsimathy:
I have acquired a smattering of late learning that under
    examination stands firm as a rock, Gibraltary or
    Plymouthy.
I have finally got it through my head
That all electric outlets are behind the sofa and under the
    bed.
I have been taught the hard way that a written gentle-
    man's agreement is more reliable than a spoken one,
Also that all your fingernails grow with inconvenient
    speed except the broken one.
I have learned that an 8:30 curtain means 8:40 if you're
    there at 8:30 but 8:30 if you're caught in a traffic jam
    caused by a rodeo cowboy roping a runaway calf,
And that the perforations on sheets of stamps are optical
    illusions: if you believe they are real you come up
    with either half a stamp or a stamp and a half.

As one who distrusts the plane,
I have had to become reconciled to the fact that wherever
   you arrive by rail the station is always at the other
   end of the train.
I guess that to dictate the percentages, to make a fortune
   out of the law of averages, is everyone's youthful
   ambition.
After a lifelong study of figures, it can't be done, con-
   cludes this once optimistic opsimathematician.

EH?

One advantage of the advancing years:
They do something to your ears.
A touch of deafness lightens one of life's heaviest chores:
Listening to bores.
Of bores I have suffered more than my portion,
And I now find that their conversation is improved by
a little distortion,
Which alleviates my malaise
At cocktail parties and buffets.
Cornered by the unkempt young woman to whom reading
Allen Ginsberg aloud to unkempt young men is fun,
My ears persuade me she said "Xenophon," not "Zen
is fun."
Thus I can loll in a wonderland more fantastic than
Alice's,
Half Anabasis, half analysis.
The female movie addict to whom the annual Oscars are
graven tablets from Hollywood's holy mountain
No longer irks me when I seem to hear her complain
that this year's award-winning song is not as good as
one of its predecessors, "Pork Loins in the Fountain."
With the aid of my aural deficiency I encounter many
happy surprises in what was once tedious social
verbosity,
And go home refreshed to listen to the TV pitchman sell-
ing me a floor polish which seems to be called
Whipped Cream, and a cigarette, the unique virtue
of which seems to be its high ferocity.

[45]

LINES FRAUGHT WITH
NAUGHT BUT THOUGHT

If you thirst to know who said, "I think, therefore I
    am," your thirst I will quench;
It was René Descartes, only what he actually said was,
    "*Je pense, donc je suis,*" because he was French.
He also said it in Latin, "*Cogito, ergo sum,*"
Just to show that he was a man of culture and not a
    tennis tramp or a cracker barrel philosophy bum.
Descartes was one of the few who think, therefore they
    are,
Because those who don't think, but are anyhow, out-
    number them by far.
If of chaos we are on the brink
It is because so many people only think that they think.
In truth, of anything other than thinking they are fonder,
Because thought requires the time and effort to reflect,
    cogitate, contemplate, meditate, ruminate and ponder.
Their minds are exposed to events and ideas but they
    have never pondered or reflected on them
Any more than motion picture screens meditate on the
    images that are projected on them.
Hence, our universal confusion,
The result of the unreasoned, or jumped at, conclusion.
People who just think that they think, they secretly think
    that thinking is grim,

And they excuse themselves with signs reading THIMK,
    or, as Descartes would have said, PEMSEZ, and
    THINK OR THWIM.
Instead of thoughts, they act on hunches and inklings,
Which are not thoughts at all, only thinklings.
Can it be because we leave to the Russians such dull
    pursuits as thinking that the red star continues to
    twinkle so?
I thinkle so.

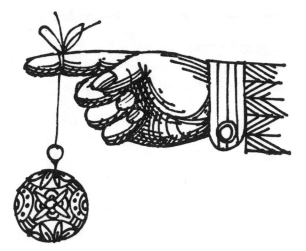

ALL'S NOËL THAT
ENDS NOËL
OR, INCOMPATIBILITY IS THE SPICE
OF CHRISTMAS

Do you know Mrs. Millard Fillmore Revere?
On her calendar, Christmas comes three hundred and
    sixty-five times a year.
Consider Mrs. Revere's Christmas spirit; no one can
    match it —
No, not Tiny Tim or big Bob Cratchit.

Even on December 26th it reveals no rifts;
She is already compiling her list of next year's gifts.
Her actions during the winter are conscientious and
    methodical,
Now snipping an advertisement from a newspaper, now
    clipping a coupon from a periodical.
In the spring she is occupied with mail-order catalogues
    from Racine and Provincetown and Richmond and
    Walla Walla,
Which offer a gallimaufry of gewgaws, gadgets, widgets,
    jiggers, trinkets, and baubles, postpaid for a dollar.
Midsummer evenings find her trudging home from clear-
    ance sales, balancing parcel upon parcel,
With blithe heart and weary metatarsal.
Soon appear the rolls of garish paper and the spools
    of gaudy ribbon,
And to describe the decline and fall of Mr. Revere it
    would take the pen of a Gibbon.
Poor Mr. Revere — such harbingers of Christmas do not
    brighten him,
They simply frighten him.
He cringes like a timid hobo when a fierce dog raises its
    hackles at him;
Wherever he steps, ribbons wind around his ankles and
    paper crackles at him.
He feels himself threatened by Christmas on all fronts;
Shakespeare had Mr. Revere in mind when he wrote,
    "Cowards die many times before their deaths; The
    valiant never taste of death but once."

These are the progressively ominous hints of impending
 doom:
First, he is forbidden to open a certain drawer, then a
 certain closet, and, finally, a certain room.
If Mr. Revere looks slightly seedy as he goes his daily
 rounds
It's because his clean shirts and socks are now out of
 bounds.
Indeed, the only reason he gets by,
He remembers previous years and has provided himself
 with haberdashery he can drip and dry.
The days of September, October, November are like
 globules of water on the forehead of a tortured pris-
 oner dropping;
Each is another day on which he has done no Christmas
 shopping.
At this point the Devil whispers that if he puts it off
 until Christmas Eve the shops will be emptier,
A thought than which nothing could be temptier,
But Christmas Eve finds him bedridden with a fever of
 nearly ninety-nine degrees, and swaddled in blankets
 up to his neck,
So on Christmas morn he has nothing for Mrs. Revere
 but a kiss and a check,
Which somehow works out fine, because she enjoys being
 kissed
And the check is a great comfort when she sits down on
 December 26th to compile her next year's list.

BRIEF LIVES IN
NOT SO BRIEF

BRIEF LIVES IN NOT SO
BRIEF — I

I yawn at the daily gossip columns,
A circling procession of tawdry names,
Publicity puffs and malicious hints,
And furtive games.

Where, then, shall I turn for honest gossip?
(I am one who on gossip thrives.)
Well, hand me over that sprightly volume,
John Aubrey's *Brief Lives*.

Here are noble foibles and durable crotchets,
Odd trifles passed over by Pepys and Evelyn,
Old bachelors' tales that outstretch old wives';
Here's gossip to revel in.

So lively they leap from Aubrey's notebooks,
Scholar and soldier, poet and peer,
That when they sneeze you cry "God bless you!"
After three hundred year.

Have ever you heard of James Bovey?
Neither had I, neither had I.
Yet he was unique among his fellows;
Aubrey tells why:
"*Red-haired men never had any kindnesse for him. In
all his Travills he was never robbed.*"

Have ever you heard of Sir Mathew Hale,
Fountain of legalistic lore?
He was Lord Chief Justice in Charles's England,
And furthermore,
"He was a great Cuckold."

Have you heard of the libel on Ben Jonson?
Neither had I, neither had I,
Till I read a remark parenthetically dropped
By my favorite spy:
"He killed Mr. Marlow, the Poet, on Bunhill, comeing
from the Green-curtain play-house."

When I doubt the genius of Edmund Waller,
Fellow-feeling banishes doubts;
I picture him with his laurels bedraggled,
A butt for louts:
"He haz but a tender weake body, but was alwayes very
temperate. They made him damnable drunke at
Somersethouse, where, at the water stayres, he fell
downe, and had a cruell fall. 'Twas pitty to use such
a sweet swan so inhumanely."

Thomas Hobbes had his day in court,
The philosopher had his dazzling day;
His friend recorded it, loyally risking
Lèse-majesté:
"The witts at Court were wont to bayte him. . . . The King
would call him the Beare: Here comes the Beare to
be bayted: (this is too low witt to be published)."

[54]

Credulous Aubrey with spaniel ears,
Friskily ranged a gamy century,
Dismissed himself and his guileless art
In a humble entry:
*"How these curiosities would be quite forgott, did not
such idle fellowes as I am putt them downe!"*

BRIEF LIVES IN NOT SO BRIEF — II

I am fond of the late poet Sir John Suckling.

He may have been no Swan of Avon, but he was a pretty
    talented Twickenham Duckling.

Along with a gift for poesy, he was possessed of ingenuity
    and effrontery;

John Aubrey tells us that he *"invented the game of Crib-
    bidge. He sent his Cards to all the Gameing places
    in the countrey,*

*Which were marked with private markes of his; he gott
    twenty thousand pounds by this way."*

Which was not then, nor is now, hay.

I suspect that sometimes the poet Suckling and the poet
    Herrick used to meet

To exchange ideas about ladies' feet.

Herrick took the first leap;

He said that Mistress Susanna Southwell's pretty feet
    crept out and drew in again like snails playing at
    bopeep.

As I have said, Suckling was no Shakespeare or Hous-
    man;

Neither was he a snail man: he was a mouse man.

So he looked up from his marked cards and loaded dice,

And said he knew a bride whose feet stole in and out
    beneath her petticoat like little mice.

As he plucked a fifth ace from under the seat,
He might have added that this bride was afraid of mice,
and succumbed to the vapours trying to run away
from her own feet.
Aubrey says of Suckling, *"He died a Batchelour,"*
Than which, considering his callous attitude toward
brides, nothing could be natchelour.

BRIEF LIVES IN NOT SO
BRIEF — III

John Aubrey had a nose for news,
In many a closet did he pry,
And on each side of his nose for news
John Aubrey had an eye for an eie.
See now his note on Francis Bacon,
Who died dishonored and forsaken:
*"He had a delicate, lively, hazel Eie; Dr. Harvey tolde
    me it was like the Eie of a viper."*

When Aubrey drank with Edmund Wyld
At the Blackmores Head in Bloomsbury,
The talk inevitably turned
To aspects of the human eie.
The satirist, Sir John Birkenhead,
Whose poems I have never read,
*"Was of midling stature, great goggli eies, not of sweet
    aspect."*

John Aubrey was a genial man;
I fancy that as he imbibed
A host of eies rolled through his brain,
All clamoring to be described.
Wouldst know the true philosopher's look?
Pause and consider Robert Hooke:
*"His head is lardge; his eie full and popping, and not
    quick; a grey eie."*

He garnered eies in town and shire
And on the winding roads between 'em,
And eies he hadn't seen himself
He snatched from people who had seen 'em.
He gives a glimpse of Sir Walter Raleigh
Not to be found in Lord Macaulay:
"Long-faced and sour eie-lidded, a kind of pigge-eie."

The strictest pedant can but praise
His brisk and lively observation,
And yet it tempted him at times
To publish idle speculation.
How will the schoolgirl in Wisconsin
Shudder to learn that rare Ben Jonson
"Had one eie lower than t'other, and bigger, like Clun
      the Player; perhaps he begott Clun."

I heard one tell who heard one tell
Who heard one tell of old John Aubrey
That when he emerged from the Blackmores Head
His eie was rather like a strawberry.

FELLOW CREATURES

[62]

THE KIPPER

For half a century, man and nipper,
I've doted on a tasty kipper,
But since I am no Jack the Ripper
I wish the kipper had a zipper.

THE REDCAP

The hunted redcap knows not peace;
His mother was frightened by a valise.
The sight of luggage seems to stun him,
And if you force a bag upon him,
Like a wary doe concealing a fawn,
He hides it till all the cabs have gone.

THE EMMET

The emmet is an ant (archaic),
The ant is just a pest (prosaic).
The modern ant, when trod upon,
Exclaims "I'll be a son-of-a-gun!"
Not so its ancestor, the emmet,
Which perished crying "Zounds!" or "Demmit!"

THE CLAM

The clam, esteemed by gourmets highly,
Is said to live the life of Riley;
When you are lolling on a piazza
Its what you are as happy as a.

THE SHRIMP

A shrimp who sought his lady shrimp
Could catch no glimpse,
Not even a glimp.
At times, translucence
Is rather a nuisance.

TO THE CHILD WHO'S FARTHER FROM THE MANNERS

OR, HOW TO BE YOUNG GRACEFULLY

Having reached the sixth of those Seven Ages,
I consider myself one of Nature's sages,
And, mumbling around my remaining tooth,
Recommend a few rules of thumb to youth.
Let's begin, as I believe we can,
With the motto, Manners makyth man.
The corollary we can't escape,
That lack of manners makyth ape.
Child, you may not be an Endymion,
But neither need you be a Simian.
Learn to accept the facts of life,
Even from your father and his wife,
Who you'll one day find were in the groove,
And, as of now, have more sense than you've.
One fact as actual as hunger
Is that older people know more than younger;
Whatever you face, they've been all through it;
Give heed when they tell you how not to do it.
They also control, for better or worse,
Strings if not of the apron, still the purse,
And if your ear I may whisper a word to,
Your elders appreciate being deferred to.

They don't appreciate yahoo whoops,
Or sidewalk monopolizing groups,
They don't appreciate costumes sloppy,
No matter which brand of Brando you copy,
Or finding themselves, at the prandial board,
Either interrupted or ignored.
They know if you go too soon too steady
You'll join them as parents before you're ready.
Though you've grown too old for your elders to spank
    you,
They like the sound of Please and Thank you.
It's not a sign of approaching senility
When they try to teach you common civility;
The civil youngster's chance is a stronger one
For not only a better life, but a longer one,
Since the driver who with Death is the flirtiest
Is the rudest, raucousest, and discourtiest,
One even Pravda could hardly applaud,
A nuisance at home and a boor abroad.
Don't sneer, or reject my words grimacefully,
I append the secret of being young gracefully;
The recipe calls for two ingredients:
Thoughtfulness and, alas, obedience.
Follow this, and you'll hear your parents purr,
For you'll be the marvel they think they were.

THE DOG

The truth I do not stretch or shove
When I state the dog is full of love.
I've also proved, by actual test,
A wet dog is the lovingest.

THE ARMADILLO

The armadillo lives inside
A corrugated plated hide.
Below the border this useful creature
Of tidy kitchens is a feature,
For housewives use an armadillo
To scour their pots, instead of Brillo.

THE CARCAJOU AND
THE KINCAJOU

They tell me of a distant zoo
Where a carcajou met a kincajou.
Full soon to savage blows they came
From laughing at each other's name.
The agile ajous fought till dark
And carc slew kinc and kinc slew carc,
And beside the conquered kincajou
Lay the carcass of the carcajou.

THE AXOLOTL

I've never met an axolotl,
But Harvard has one in a bottle,
Perhaps — and at the thought I shiver —
The very villain from Fall River,
Where Lizzie Borden took an axolotl
And gave her mother forty whaxolotl.

DON'T BITE THE HAND
THAT PUTS ITS FOOT
IN YOUR MOUTH

"The district leader is the arm of Tammany that does the leg work." — A district leader, as heard in a radio interview.

Aloof, alone upon his thone
Sits the sapient head of Tammany,
A noble head, the brain pan filled
With godly thoughts, not Mammony.
Of nepotism knows he naught,
Or barratry, or simony,
But hopeful plans a permanent,
A benevolent hegemony.
He dedicates his intellect
To the cause of party harmony,
And mental auditions daily holds
For an orchestrated nominee.
His primary function he cannot change
To physical from cerebral,
Any more than the leopard will change its spots,
Or its natural stripes the zebra'll,
So when there's need of a fine fat cat, or a goose for
    golden egg work,
He calls the district leader in, the arm that does the leg
    work.

Perceptive of the people's will
Is the sapient head of Tammany,
Reacting to every change of wind

Like a sensitive anemone.
He longs for a numerologist,
Or a crystal-gazing Romany,
For that damnable bore is here again,
An election Anno Domini.
When the valid votes are counted,
Will his future be feast or faminy?
Will he eat his lunch in a one-arm joint,
Or in a swell *estaminet*?
For Fiorello's footsteps
Still echo in the corridor;
Reform is a horrid word enough,
But Fusion is even horrider.
So, faced with making a circular hole and a quadrilateral
    peg work,
He sends for the district leader, the arm that does the leg
    work.

The sapient head of Tammany
Provides a lesson for us:
The only creature whose arms are legs
Is the greedy octopus.

CAPERCAILLIE, AVE
ATQUE VAILLIE

One letter from a long correspondence on the capercaillie in the English magazine *Country Life* is headed
"How To Outwit The Capercaillie" and reads, in part:
". . . the cock capercaillie is blind and deaf during the last
part of each 'verse' of his love song, the part described
by Mr. Richmond as sounding 'like a polar bear splash-
ing into a swimming pool.' . . . Between verses and during
the first two parts of them (the 'kek kek kek' and
'whoosh'), however, the cock is most alert. . . ."

Spring, the sweet Spring, is the year's pleasant king;
Then blooms each thing, then maids dance in a ring,
Cold doth not sting, capercaillie then doth sing —
Kek kek kek, whoosh, kek kek kek, whoosh!

Sings he no cuckoo, jug-jug, pu-we, to-witta-woo,
Trills doth he eschew, lark song and tereu,
Hen doth he woo with wild Highland cockadoo —
Kek kek kek, whoosh, kek kek kek, whoosh!

The truant from school doth think to hear a ghoul,
Bee-stung bear in pool, or scold on ducking stool,
Nay, nay, young fool! Here cries a ravished soul —
Kek kek kek, whoosh, kek kek kek, whoosh!

To bird of caution rid, with rival now outbid,
Comes, as to Duncan did, stop't ear and closèd lid,
And archer, slyly hid, transfixes him amid
Kek kek kek, whoosh, and kek kek kek, whoosh.

Farewell, poor cock, which died a laughingstock —
Yet thy pibroch doth lately run amok,
While chicks of strange flock chant, as they roll and rock,
Kek kek kek, whoosh, kek kek kek, whoosh!

THE PANDIT

OR, PERHAPS WE WERE WRONG ABOUT
THAT, BUT AS LONG AS WE'RE
BEING FRANK . . .

Just how shall we define a pandit?
It's not a panda, not a bandit,
But rather a Pandora's box
Of sophistry and paradox.
Though Oxford gave it a degree
It maintains its neutrality
By quietly hating General Clive
As hard as if he were alive.
On weighty international questions
It's far more Christian than most Christians;
It's ever eager, being meek,
To turn somebody else's cheek.
Oft has it said all men are brothers
And set that standard up for others,
Yet as it spoke it gerrymandered,
Proclaiming its private Pakistandard.
The neutral pandit walks alone
And, if abroad it casts a stone,
It walks impartial to the last,
Ready at home to stone a caste.
Abandon I for now the pandit;
I fear I do not understand it.

[81]

THE MIRACULOUS
COUNTDOWN

Let me tell you of Dr. Faustus Foster.
Chloe was lost, but he was loster.
He was what the world for so long has missed,
A truly incompetent scientist.
His morals were good and his person cleanly,
He had skied at Peckett's and rowed at Henley.
The only liquor that touched his lips
He drew through pipettes with filter tips.
He could also recite, in his modest manner,
The second verse of The Star-Spangled Banner.
Yet, to his faults we must not be blinded;
He was ineluctably woolly-minded.
When his further deficiencies up are summed,
He was butter fingered and margarine thumbed.
You'd revoke the license of any rhymer
Who ranked him with Teller and Oppenheimer.
It took him, and here your belief I beg,
Twenty minutes to boil a three-minute egg,
Which will give you a hint as to what went on
Whenever he touched a cyclotron.
There wasn't a problem he feared to face,
From smashing atoms to conquering space,

And, should one of his theories expire,
He had other ions in the fire,
Even walking to work to save his carfare
For tackling bacteriological warfare.
For years he went to no end of bother
To explode this planet or reach another.
A more ambitious, industrious savant
You may have encountered; I know I haven't.
One Christmas Eve he was tired and irked,
He had shot the works and nothing worked.
"I'd sell my soul," he cried to the night,
"To have one experiment come out right."
No sooner said than his startled eyes
Saw a ghostly stranger materialize,
Who, refraining from legalistic jargon,
Announced, "You have got yourself a bargain.
Here's a pact with iron-clad guarantees;
Sign here, in the usual fluid, please."
Faustus disdained to quibble or linger,
He merely remarked, as he pricked his finger,
"It had better be good, your *quid pro quo*;
My blood is especially fine type O."
(Always in character, come what may
He was down in his doctor's records as A.)
A snicker was heard from the stranger weird,
Then he snatched the parchment and disappeared.
Faustus was filled with wild surmise
And roseate dreams of the Nobel Prize,
Now certain to drop in his lap with awful ease,
He thought, with the aid of Mephistopheles.

Behold him now in his laboratory,
A modern Merlin, hell-bent for glory.
With a flourish worthy of the Lunts
He triggered every project at once.
Intercontinental ballistic missiles
Blasted the air with roars and whistles,
Rockets punctured the midnight clear,
And the atmosphere and the stratosphere.
Before the human eye could absorb it
A giant satellite entered orbit.
With the germ's equivalent of a howl
The bacteria issued forth to prowl.
Faustus shouted with joy hysterical,
And was then struck dumb as he watched a miracle.
He gazed aghast at his handiwork
As every experiment went berserk.
The bacteria, freed from their mother mold,
Settled down to cure the common cold.
Distant islanders sang Hosanna
As nuclear fall-out turned to manna.
Rockets, missiles and satellite
Formed a flaming legend across the night.
From Cape Canaveral clear to the Isthmus
The monsters spelled out Merry Christmas,
Penitent monsters whose fiery breath
Was rich with hope instead of death.
Faustus, the clumsiest of men,
Had butter-fingered a job again.
I've told you his head was far from level;
He thought he had sold his soul to the devil,

When he'd really sold it, for heaven's sake,
To his guardian angel by mistake.
When geniuses all in every nation
Hasten us towards obliteration,
Perhaps it will take the dolts and geese
To drag us backward into peace.

THE UNSEEING EYE:
THE TRAVEL DIARY OF A
NON-OBSERVER

PARADISE FOR SALE

DORSET — 8 miles DORCHESTER
In the valley of the River Piddle.
KIDDLES FARM, PIDDLETRENTHIDE
A SMALL MIXED FARM
WITH SMALL PERIOD FARMHOUSE
DINING/LIVING ROOM, KITCHEN
3 BED ROOMS, BATHROOM
    —Adv. in Country Life.

Had I the shillings, pounds, and pence,
I'd pull up stakes and hie me hence;
I'd buy that small mixed farm in Dorset,
Which has an inglenook and faucet —
Kiddles Farm,
Piddletrenthide,
In the valley of the River Piddle.

I'd quit these vehement environs
Of diesel fumes and horns and sirens,
This manic, fulminating ruction
Of demolition and construction,
For Kiddles Farm,
Piddletrenthide,
In the valley of the River Piddle.

Yes, quit for quietude seraphic
Con Edison's embrangled traffic,

To sit reflecting that the skylark,
Which once was Shelley's, now is my lark,
At Kiddles Farm,
Piddletrenthide,
In the valley of the River Piddle.

I'm sure the gods could not but bless
The man who lives at that address,
And revenue agents would wash their hands
And cease to forward their demands
To Kiddles Farm,
Piddletrenthide,
In the valley of the River Piddle.

Oh, the fiddles I'd fiddle,
The riddles I'd riddle,
The skittles I'd scatter,
The winks I would tiddle!
Then hey diddle diddle!
I'll jump from the griddle
And live out my days
To the end from the middle
On Kiddles Farm,
Piddletrenthide,
In the valley of the River Piddle.

THE AZORES

An Azore is an isle volcanic
Whose drivers put me in a panic.
The English expression "Slow down, please"
Means "Step on the gas!" in Portuguese.
An Azore is a beauty spot?
I don't know whether it is or not.
While racing round it hell-for-leather,
My eyelids were always jammed together.

AMSTERDAM, ROTTERDAM,
AND THE HAGUE

The Dutchmen are their own best pals,
They're satisfied with their own canals,
So their galleries lack one major menace —
Those everlasting views of Venice.

MADEIRA

Madeira is the home of wineries
And extremely expensive embroidered fineries.
I seem to sense a relation tender
Between vintner and embroidery vender.
Free sample sippings of the grape
Inflate the tourist to a shape
In which, by the time he's embroiled in the embroidery
    imbroglio,
He will pay for a dozen doilies the price of an authentic
    First Folio.

MOROCCO

The bus to Marrakech, Morocco,
Traverses landscapes simply socko.
The agricultural economy
Suggests the Book of Deuteronomy.
The machine has not replaced the mammal,
And everything is done by camel.
I hope I never learn what flesh
I ate that day in Marrakech,
But after struggling with a jawful
I thought it tasted humpthing awful.

TRANSATLANTIC TRANSPORTS

LONDON

The London taxi is a relic
For which my zeal is evangelic.
It's designed for people wearing hats,
And not for racing on Bonneville Flats.
A man can get out, or a lady in;
When you sit, your knees don't bump your chin.
The driver so deep in the past is sunk
That he'll help you with your bags and trunk;
Indeed, he is such a fuddy-duddy
That he calls you Sir instead of Buddy.

PARIS

The independent Parisian hackie
Is bent on proving he's no man's lackey.
As railroads feel about commuters,
As Odysseus felt toward Penelope's suitors,
As landlords feel about repairs,
That's how he feels toward potential fares.
They inspire him with horrendous hates
Which into hunger he sublimates,
So when you hail him he's pleased as Punch
To spit in your eye and go to lunch.

SWITZERLAND

I'm not over-particular
About travel vehicular,
Except of the kind I find too perpendicular.
I may perish abroad, but not on a funicular.
The bobsled is racy,
The ski even racier;
Myself, I have found
If you travel by glacier
You can gather the edelweiss much efficacier.

MALAGA

Malaga's on the Iberian peninsula,
Where very few natives are named Van Rensselaer.
The trams are linked together in Malaga
Like Mason and Dixon, or Shean and Gallagher.
They rattle through the town at random,
Not arm in arm, at random tandem.
The time they traveled abreast in Malaga
It was worse than the battle of Trafalagar,
So trams no longer travel abreast,
Having found tandem tramdom best.

VENICE

The Venetian who wishes to spark
Can't say, Drive around Central Park.
He coaxes her into a gondola
When he wishes to woo and fondola,
But after the rice and confetti
They ride on the *vaporetti*.

[97]

MOSCOW

Over the Volga and through the snow
Away to Babushka's house we go,
Party members aboard a troika,
Whistling Beethoven's Eroica,
Or chattering gaily in a droshky,
While chewing blinis and piroshki,
And eschewing Molotov melancholia
And morbid thoughts of Outer Mongolia.

AS GAUGUIN SAID
TO SADIE THOMPSON,
YOU PRONOUNCE IT,
I'LL PAINT IT

It was not really stout Cortez who stood silent
    upon a peak in Darien, it was stout Balboa;
It was a misty day, and he couldn't see Samoa.
Nowadays Samoa can be seen by anybody with
    the price of a ship or plane ticket, or who
    can build his own raft,
As can Tahiti, Pago Pago, Bali, Fiji and
    other Pacific paradises over which tourists go daft.

At the prospect of visiting these oft-visited
    garden spots I am not one jot or whit elated;
Rather would I seek out those strange-sounding
    geographical pinpoints by which the ear
    as well as the eye is titillated.
In the course of titillating my ears
I have been cruising through the Hydrographic Office
    of the United States Navy Department's *Gazetteers*.
Who that revels in lingual judo
Could resist the challenge of the rocks
    of MUDOGOMUBURAMARUDAVEMUDO?
Doesn't it fill you with euphoria
To think of PUKAPUKA, where the sahib
    sahibs gather to drink the health of Queen Victoria?
You can rest your tongue with YAP and BAM and KUKU,
Then work up through MOG MOG and
    KWAMKWAM and BORA BORA to
    BOHIGUMAGUMA and BONGLELONGDANGO
    and ANIGIGICHAIRUKKU.
If you couldn't get a redcap wouldn't you
    be happy to drag a bag
Through BLUPBLUP or BUM BUM or BAGABAG?
Finally, with the golden sand below and the
    golden moon above you,
You could relax among the golden girls of
    SONGSONG or LUVULUVU,
Which conclusion leads me to believe, on the whole,
That the garden spots of the Pacific were
    named by those who write the lyrics for rock and roll,

Or perhaps they simply seem somewhat out of focus
Because I come from a land of conventional
     names, such as Walla Walla, Oshkosh,
     Skaneateles and Hohokus.

DON'T LOOK NOW,
BUT THERE'S SOMETHING
BEHIND THE CURTAIN

Life is more exciting for greenhorns than for tired-eyed
old fogies,
Because greenhorns can still shudder at bugbears and
bogies.
Adventure is closer to your young Philip Sidney
Than to the executive vice-president who boasts a color-
TV set in every room and a swimming-pool-shaped
kidney.
How vividly I remember, and still with a slight inclina-
tion to scream,
My first encounter with the phrase *"société anonyme."*
Surely the French language contains no other term that
so smacks of sinister devilment,
That so reduces an alien morale to a state of dishevelment.
I skulked through Paris as in an evil dream
While kiosk and hoarding hissed at me, *"Société anonyme!
Société anonyme!"*
Who were these nameless ones? The Maffia? The Ku-
Klux Klan? The Sign of Four?
When would their hooded figures come scratching at my
door?

Houp-là, the relief, and, *hélas,* the anticlimax and humili-
ation
To learn that *"société anonyme"* means plain old "corpora-
tion."
Life is indeed a seesaw
On which the shrug too soon succeeds the *frisson.*

OUR CITY, OUR CITIZENS
OR, PATIENCE AND FORTITUDE

THE VILLAGE

What walls them from the world of men,
These unkempt anthropoids?
Though fifty sages call it Zen,
I plump for adenoids.

THE GOLD COAST

High up along Park Avenue
A bit of Moscow comes in view.
Here, after a day at United Nations
Of dutiful denunciations,
Reside the bluebloods of the Reds,
True dialectic thoroughbreds.
A group my tiresome Cousin Emlyn
Refers to as *la crème de la Kremlin.*

THE AMPUTATORS

There's one I care for even less
Than him who toasts me with "God bless!"
The TV weather maiden snappy
Who waves good night with "Have a happy!"

THE CAFÉ PRESS AGENT

Nose-cone heiress "Bubbles" de Radzovitch
Claims that an adult Western is one in which . . .
"Googie" Friganza claims that an author of note
Is changing his name to Kennedy Capote . . .
Count "Vovo" Rienzi comes up with a brand-new drink,
The Psychiatrist, one sip and your head will shrink . . .
Heard at the Snorkel, while visiting to and fro:
"It isn't how much you know, but who you know" . . .
Crag Torso, here on a picture-plugging pitch,
Claims that an adult Western is one in which . . .

THEATRE HOUR

The hotel doorman's frantic whistle
Makes rugged taxi drivers bristle.
The doormen chittering like grackles
Only raise the hacky's hackles.
Contemptuously stares the cabby
Like a bobcat at a tabby,
Then with derisive farewell honks
Heads happily homeward to the Bronx.
That's why, my children, I'm afraidy
That you'll be late for "My Fair Lady."

CITY GREENERY

If you should happen after dark
To find yourself in Central Park,
Ignore the paths that beckon you
And hurry, hurry to the zoo,
And creep into the tiger's lair.
Frankly, you'll be safer there.

THE COMIC

Children demand the tale as told before,
The slightest alteration they deplore.
The comic, by the time he is the rage,
Has learned the night-club patron's mental age.
So, infinite variety is dead,
And repetition rules the roost instead.
Reaching the Copa from less opulent climes
Now one man in his part plays many times.

IMPRESSIONS OF SUBURBIA
BY ONE WHO HAS NEVER
BEEN THERE

OR, ALL I KNOW IS WHAT I SEE
IN THE ADS

Suburbia is a modern Utopia,
Of gracious living a cornucopia.
The average family income, I hear,
Is twenty-five thousand dollars a year.
Station wagons adorn the valleys and ridges,
And the sports cars travel in swarms, like midges.
Here are gardens where no one weeds or delves,
Where tomatoes and tulips raise themselves,
And, should furnace or freezer act less than dandy,
There's always a quaint old handy-man handy.
The summer weekends are always cool
Round the barbecue grill and the swimming pool,
And in winter the family hovers in glee
O'er the Hi-fi set and the color TV.
With the joys of Nature in such propinquity
There's an absence of juvenile delinquity.
The children (each home has two and a third)
Are the kind that are seen and never heard,

So at nightfall instead of the city's turbulence
You hear a kind of soothing suburbulence
As the young obediently hit the hay
And parents drive off to the P.T.A.
Such is my vision of Suburbia,
Where I'd rather live than in Russia or Serbia.

A DAY ON A CRUISE

OR, WHAT A DAY! WHAT A CRUISE!

How do we start the day on a cruise?
By picking up *The Neptune News*,
Which rustles under the cabin door
And expires of shame upon the floor.
You look for world events, or sports,
And find idiot scraps, distorted orts,
Ephemeral items and cosmic terrors
In a mishmash of typographical errors;
Moscob and Washingtov haven't ceased
To disagree in the Muddle East,
And Princeton, in a porkskin duel,
Has gained two tuckdowns over Yule;
You can't grow archids in Antarctica,
And prices are slomping on the stock ticker.
The only part that is printed clear
Is the chart of the day's compulsory cheer,
A maelstrom of fun that will not end
Till maelstrom and femaelstrom blend.

Comes a whoop like the Sioux in pursuit of the Senecas,
It's the happy cry of the calisthenickers;
Then those nautical noises that Masefield finds fetching—
Knees creaking, and rubber stretching,

As the Early Birdies reach for their toes,
Which they've not even seen since when, God knows.

Now for the tourneys, that triple menace,
Ping-pong, shuffleboard, and deck tennis.
Like a press gang the stewards, a solid wall of them,
Try to enlist you in one or all of them;
Why can't they just bring your crackers and broth
And leave you to snooze like a three-toed sloth?
You've paid your way on this thousand-dollar ship,
You're not here on an athletic scholarship;
Besides, the girls who infest the tournaments
Are usually not their sex's ornaments.

The afternoon assumes various shapes,
But mostly mummery and japes.
This is the hour of the cruise director,
As grimly jolly as Marley's specter,
Observing one unswerving rule,
That everybody must play the fool.
The deck is scoured of sour-faced Scrooges
And left to his groups of eager stooges,
With each respectable uncle and auntie
Ready to play at faun and bacchante.
Observe the gents, though your plasma curdles,
In a race to don their spouses' girdles;
The winner, no stranger to alcohol,
Is awarded a saucy sailor doll.
Then the ladies, clad in shorts and halters,
Describing whom description falters,

With girlish giggles and raucous hoots
Cram themselves into union suits.
The band strikes up its merriest tunes
While they stuff the union suits with balloons,
And the gents discover, by means of pins,
Where lady ends and balloon begins.
If you'll pardon a pun of picayunacy,
Let's draw a veil over such balloonacy.
These infant minds in adult corpuses,
Let's leave them to the gulls and porpoises,
Let's take a little trip inside,
Where soberer souls are occupied.
In the smoking room there's a tingle spinal,
The bridge tournament enters the semifinal,
And the lounge provides an enthralling lecture
On Neo-Mycenaean architecture.
Like the setting sun, too long we've tarried,
For tongues are parched and throats are arid.
Come one, come all, drink free and hearty,
This is the captain's cocktail party.
Irresistibly moves the ravenous horde
On hors d'oeuvres, antipasto or smorgasbord;
They scream for martinis and Bloody Marys
As if calling hogs across the prairies,
And no one admits they've had enough
When the browsing and sluicing is on the cuff.
Behold the captain, unhappy and warm;
All day he has prayed in vain for a storm.
Now he's trapped by a large and tipsy Lorelei
Behind whose bifocals gleams an immoral eye;

When she asks if he'll let her steer his boat,
He restrains his fingers from her throat,
But his face turns red, and his stare gets starier,
And he scuttles behind the language barrier.

The swollen crowd is suddenly thinner;
The bugle has blown for the gala dinner,
A riot of cummerbunds and organdy,
And jeroboams of sparkling burgundy,
And false noses and comic cravats,
And toy trumpets and paper hats,
And drums and rattles and castanets,
And confetti all over the crêpes Suzettes,
A sight unequaled, I do believe,
Save in Times Square on New Year's Eve.

Before the dancing, we turn to Bingo,
Which on a cruise has a special lingo;
When to fill your card you're the first in the room,
Instead of Bingo! you shout, Kaboom!
I know a man whose luck was hot,
Three times he would have won the pot,
But he was an individual whom
Was far too stuffy to holler, Kaboom!
One hour later his grandmama
Won the dancing prize with her cha-cha-cha.

Well, that's how people behave on a cruise;
Everybody, that is, except me and youse.

TABLE TALK

THE POMEGRANATE

The hardest fruit upon this planet
Is easily the ripe pomegranate.
I'm halfway through the puzzle game
Of guessing how it got its name.
The pome part turns my cowlick hoary,
But the granite is self-explanatory.

ICEBERG LETTUCE

I cheerfully forgive my debtors,
But I'll never pardon iceberg lettuce,
A pallid package of rigidity,
A globe of frozen insipidity.
I hope I'll never be so punchy
As to relish my salad crisp and crunchy,
Yet garden lettuce with leafy head
Is as hard to get as unsliced bread.

TARRAGON

There are certain people
Whom certain herbs
The good digestion of disturbs.
Henry VIII
Divorced Catherine of Aragon
Because of her reckless use of tarragon.

THE CODFISH

The codfish is a staple food
For which I'm seldom in the mood.
This fish is such an utter loss
That people eat it with egg sauce,
One of the odd fish codfish habits
I leave to the Lowells and the Cabots.

THE BEEFBURGER

In mortal combat I am joined
With monstrous words wherever coined
"Beefburger" is a term worth hating,
Both fraudulent and infuriating,
Contrived to foster the belief
That only beefburgers are made of beef,
Implying with shoddy flim and flam
That hamburgers are made of ham.

ASPIC

What a pity that aspic
Doesn't rhyme with elastic,
Because gee whiz,
It is.

MUSTARD

I'm mad about mustard —
Even on custard.

HOLLANDAISE

I sing the praise of Hollandaise,
A sauce supreme in many ways.
Not only is it a treat to us
When ladled on asparagus,
But I would shudder to depict
A world without Eggs Benedict.

MENU MACABRE

Let us now get away from praise of anti-smoke pollution
    measures and plans for noise abatements,
Let us now praise famous gourmets and their equally
    famous ante-mortem statements.
The preoccupation of the gourmet with good food is
    psychological,
Just as the preoccupation of the White Russian with
    Dark Eyes is balalaikalogical.
The gourmet eats for the moment, because what at his
    back does he always hear?
The Great Headwaiter with *l'addition* hurrying near.
How then do gourmets approach the bottom of life's bill
    of fare?
Some with foresight, some with false courage, and some
    with *sang-froid* of the most debonair.
In the first group, Isaiah, a connoisseur of pottage,
Especially in his dottage.
That his future messes of pottage were numbered he had
    a foreboding,
And he said, Let us eat and drink; for tomorrow we shall
    die, a message that needs no decoding.
In the second, Sydney Smith; Fate cannot harm me, I
    have dined today, was his remark,
A perfect example of whistling in the dark.

Now the third group:

Consider Raoul, Comte de Gruelle, epicure, sybarite, *bon vivant,* and world authority on soup.

He went on an expedition in search of herbs for the ultimate in exotic seasoning,

And he was captured by cannibals in a country which the State Department requests me to call Ruritania, through obvious political reasoning.

As he stood in the cauldron with water scalding his fundament

He sampled each new added condiment.

When the broth reached his lips he smacked them heartily, and his last words, at 212°F.,

Were, My compliments to the chef.

WHICH CAME FIRST,
OBEISANCE OR OBESITY?

You'd be sitting pretty, with nothing in the world to
　　trouble you,
Were it not that someone quite high up in your family
　　is quite high up in the I.O.O.P.W.,
So at mealtime your heart with apprehension is filled,
Because the I.O.O.P.W. is the International Order of
　　Plate Watchers — a powerful and articulate guild.
A Plate Watcher, I need hardly state,
Watches everybody else's plate.
She begins with over-hospitality
And ends up with aggressive frugality.
She urges people to help themselves far beyond their
　　capacity, to pile mashed potatoes on Yorkshire pud-
　　ding, and apple pandowdy on shoofly pie,
And then fixes them with a waste-not, want-not eye.
She smelleth the laggard afar off; she saith among the
　　diners, Ha, ha!
And woe betide him who has attempted to conceal be-
　　neath the cutlery one ultimate tiny little *petit pois*.
Indeed, woe doubly betides that reluctant regaler,
For he has been ordered to watch his weight by both his
　　physician and, what is more important, his tailor.
I recommend to any ardent debate watcher
A seat at table presided over by a Plate Watcher married
　　to a weight watcher.

SING A SONG OF
TASTE BUDS

The wine snob is so well established,
His clichés are so widely published,
He's so ingenuous in his worship
Of his own erudite connoisseurship,

He gives himself such harmless pleasure
That you humor him in modest measure
And sometimes ask him how to tell
An honest from a great Moselle,
As one who tosses from his rocker
A ball to please an eager cocker.
To paraphrase Aesop's pithy parlarance,
Familiarity breeds tolerance.

The gin snob, on the other hand,
Has lately burst upon the land.
More brash than the oenologist
Who judges grapes, he judges grist,
Presumably grading in his brain
The varying vintage years of grain.
This man of the world can find no merit
In any domestic neutral spirit.
No Kansas maidens, skirts a-ripple,
Shall tread the kernels for his tipple,
Nebraska, no, nor Ioway,
Provide it body and bouquet;
The gin employed to make him squiffy
Must be distilled near Thames or Liffey.
His own, his native strong drink he mocks,
Demanding Old Hogarth on the rocks
Until tomorrow or next week
Old Muttoneater becomes more chic.

I prefer a twice-told tale of vineyards
To a guided tour through alien ginyards.

THE PAID ATTENDANCE

DECLINE AND FALL
OF A ROMAN UMPIRE

I sing of Tony Caesar, a big league arbiter of unimpeach-
    able repute
Except for one impeacher, who was a beaut.
Tony dreaded each new season because whenever behind
    third base at the Stadium he took his stand
This impeacher was on hand.
He had a cowbell and a bull voice,
And his vocabulary, though limited, was far from choice.
It beat on Tony's ears like a savage drum:
Caesar, ya big bum ya, you're nothing but a big bum!
Sometimes he would crummily roar, Caesar, you ain't no
    umpire,
You're a bumpire!
Sometimes he would roar something even crummier,
But mostly he just roared, Oh ya big bum, ya big bum ya!

Tony was really as saintly a man as Dr. Jekyll,
But the more his heckler continued to heckle,
Why the more he began to feel like Mr. Hyde,
Until one day he decided to have his heckler private-
    eyed,

And when the private eye turned in his report, well the next time Tony was called a bum,
He walked over to his tormentor and mildly said, Come, come!
I am reliably informed that you have one wife in Brooklyn, one in the Bronx, and a lady friend in Queens;
Your first conviction was for robbing a blind vendor of newspapers and magazines;
Your other offenses range from drunk and disorderly to pocket-picking, automobile theft and arson,
As well as making off with the poor box after brutally assaulting the parson.
I suggest, sir, that you take heed;
Who is calling whom a bum, yes, whom indeed?
To which the snarled reply was, Aah, get your eye out of my thumb;
I'm calling *you* a bum, ya big bum!
Tony gave up and abandoned the big leagues for the Little League and changed his name to Tittelbaum,
And he is happy now because the spectators only call him a little bum.

CHAMPIONS AND CHIMPIONS

Once there was a football coach who was called Hush-
    mouth McGunn,
Because his favorite expression was "Hush mah mouth,"
    a deed that was aspired to by many but accom-
    plished by none.
To his identity no sports lover needs a clue;
He was coach of the Juggling Juggernauts of Jericho U.
Rarely did the Juggernauts let Hushmouth down,
Thrice had they brought him the Rose Bowl crown,
And there were even greater triumphs beyond;
The fourth crown was dangling ready to be donned.
Simultaneously with his acceptance of the Bowl bid came
    the choices for All-American,
And of the 22 positions on the offensive and defensive
    platoons, every one was occupied by a Jerichan.
Their prospective opponents, the University of Whither
    California, bore so little resemblance to a football
    team that when they appeared on What's My Line
    they baffled even the omniscient John Daly,
But guess what, the entire 22 All-American Jerichans
    were disabled in a plane crash while headed for
    the Ed Sullivan Show, the news of which at Whither
    California was welcomed gaily.

At Jericho U. an air of doom is prevalent;

Hush, hush, whisper who dares, Hushmouth McGunn is saying his prayers, or the equivalent.

To address him is imprudent,

But sudden his curiosity is aroused by the approach of an unfamiliar object, a student,

Who says, Sir, it is only a humble student with a 4-bit wager on the Bowl game who at your feet devoutly kneels,

But have you heard the theory that a dozen apes playing with a dozen typewriters could in time reproduce every book ever written, from Homer's to Norman Vincent Peale's?

The coach for once cannot even say, Hush mah mouth, he says, Gadzooks!

Who wants books?

The student flinches but persists, Sir, suppose 22 apes were locked up with diagrams of plays devised by such masters as yourself and Wilkinson and Paul Brown and Weeb Ewbank and Papa Bear George Halas,

Chances are they might learn them verbatim and burst on the world like the aurora borealis. . . .

Came the New Year, and I tell you there hasn't been such an afternoon in Pasadena

Since Baby Leroy choked on his farina.

Jericho's workouts had been secret, and rumors were contradictory;

Hushmouth's only statement was that his squad of third-stringers had vowed not to shave until after victory.

You could hardly call it a game,

Whither California was overwhelmed by the best features
of the Browns and Oklahoma and Notre Dame.

They never knew by what they would be hit,

A split-T or a banana split,

And they were driven out of their mind

When a rip in the Juggernaut fullback's pants revealed
an iridescent red and blue behind.

The score was 77-0 at the half, and Hushmouth's heart
sang;

In the dressing room he delivered a joyously excited har-
angue.

When he returned to the bench his only thought was of
the swathe he would cut among the ladies

When the grateful alumni fulfilled their promise of that
sports Mercedes.

Alas, he had forgotten that the simian mind cannot dis-
criminate,

And among the diagrams he had gathered for his pupils
were a few old Harvard plays that he had neglected
to eliminate.

Jericho bowed, 77 to 78, and Hushmouth is still driving
last year's Cadillac convertible,

But his spirits are unhurtable.

He had grown to love his hairy little charges, and often
when bowling with his fellow keglers

He proudly exclaims, Hush mah mouth, those monks
weren't no athaletes, but their scholastic average was
two points higher than the reg'lars!

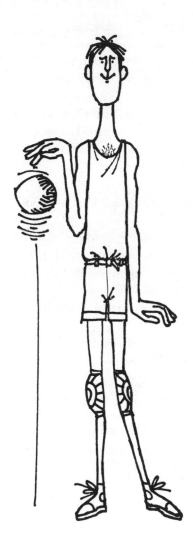

—AND DON'T FORGET WEIGHT-LIFTING, SHOT-PUTTING, AND THE LADIES' JUNIOR BACKSTROKE CHAMPIONSHIP

All winter long, yes, every day,
I throw the sporting page away,
I turn my faithful radio off
And grimly settle down to scoff,
Since contests that as sport I list,
In wintertime do not exist.
If Mr. Gallup me is polling
He will not tally a vote for bowling;
Despite our brief Olympic radiance,
Hockey belongs to the Canadians;
But chiefly am I unbeguiled
By Dr. Naismith's monster child,
Basketball is not a sport,
Not even as a last resort —
A game indulged in by giraffes
And only good for scornful laughs,
All whistle-blowings and palaverages
And scores that read like Dow-Jones averages.
Only Harlem's unique Globetrotters,
As comic as seals and slick as otters,

Find its pretensions are grotesque
And treat it purely as burlesque.
But hark! A hint from softer climes
Of past and future golden times!
In Phoenix and St. Petersburg
The rookie generates the erg,
And Vero Beach and Sarasota
Of embryo Ruths can boast their quota.
The airwaves now begin to tingle
As grapefruit knights in tourney mingle;
Again the happiness pills I know
Of sporting page and radio.
Home is the exile, home the rover,
The storm of basketballs is over;
I sail serenely into harbor
With Phil Rizzuto and Red Barber.

THE MOTHER TONGUE

MOTHER ISN'T WELL

I do not like the sound of "additive,"
The current video pitchman's fadditive.
From scrutiny of a thousand screens
I've now decided what it means:
You add a syllable, as in "moderen,"
"Prince Charels," "westeren," or "squaderon."
The additive, as a matter of factitive,
Logically leads to the subtractitive,
By eminent announcers endorsed,
In which the forest becomes the forst.
When I hear an orange called an ornch
I feel forgotten and forlornch —

Yet whom am I to cavil thus?
My own faults are preposterous.
I've caught me, even without imbibery,
Referring to my reference libary.
Occasionally, if still you follow me,
I prefer to pronounce the "P" in Ptolemy.
I also admit that almost half the
Time I omit the "h" in naphtha.

LAMENTS FOR A DYING LANGUAGE

What's the monster of this week?
"Mystique" —
A noun that in its current arcane use leaves me frigid,
Since it is not to be found in either the O.E.D. or Webster's Unabridgèd.
It is primarily the invention of the mystagogues of esoteric criticism, so it means whatever they choose,
But I will give you an example of what I think they think it means, only from the domain of a different muse.
I recently heard on the air a song in which the lover states that the loved one is his idea
Of a band of angels singing "Ave Maria."
This is not only a metaphor unique,
It is also an example of the songwriter's mystique at its peak.

II

Someone comes up with a linguistic gimmick,
And thousands flock to mimic.
This noisy age, when big loud bangs give way to bangs louder and bigger still,
And admirals, congressmen, and minor government officials pop off at will,
Gives us two gimmicks that reflect our minds' corrosion:
"Crash program" and "explosion."

See here the population explosion, the freedom explosion,
   the Broadway and off-Broadway incest-theme explosion, the explosion of British secretaries in offices
   of grandiose pretensions,
And there the crash program for defense, for space explor-
   ation, for a third major league, for nominating the
   candidates previous to the conventions.
With each successive bang my hopes grow limper
That the world's end will be a simple whimper.

III

In the nice-minded Department of Prunes and Prisms,
It's I for you
And euphemisms.
Hence the phrase I would eagerly jettison:
"Senior citizen."
Shall we retranslate
Joel 2, 28?
To the sociologist squeamish
The words "Your old men shall dream dreams" are less
   than beamish,
So "Your senior citizens shall dream dreams" it shall
   henceforth be,
Along with Hemingway's "The Senior Citizen and the
   Sea."
I, though no Joel, prophesy that someday while the
   senior citizens are projecting the image of an age-
   adjusted social group,
The old men will rise up and knock them for a loop.

[147]

IV

Those authors I can never love
Who write, "It fit him like a glove."
Though baseballs may be hit, not "hitted,"
The past of "fit" is always "fitted."
The sole exception worth a *haricot*
Is "Joshua fit de battle ob Jericho."

V

Coin brassy words at will, debase the coinage;
We're in an if-you-cannot-lick-them-join age,
A slovenliness-provides-its-own-excuse age,
Where usage overnight condones misusage.
Farewell, farewell to my beloved language,
Once English, now a vile orangutanguage.

JUST HOW LOW CAN
A HIGHBROW GO WHEN
A HIGHBROW LOWERS
HIS BROW?

Take the intellectual prig;
For his pretensions I do not care a whit or a fig.
I am content that he should know what name Achilles
assumed among the women, and do his crosswords in
Esperanto,
And ostentatiously comprehend the inner meaning of
Pound's obscurest canto.
It does not disturb me that he can distinguish between
"flaunt" and "flout," and "costive" and "costate,"
What does disturb me is his black-sheep brother, the
intellectual prig apostate.
Such a one is so erudite that he frequently thinks in
Aramaic,
But he expresses himself in slang long passé in Passaic.
His signature is purple ink in an illegible curlicue,
And he compares baseball to ballet, and laments the
passing of burlesque, which he refers to as burlicue.
He has a folksy approach to the glory that was Greece,
And professes to find more social and sociological sig-
nificance in "Li'l Abner" than in *War and Peace*.

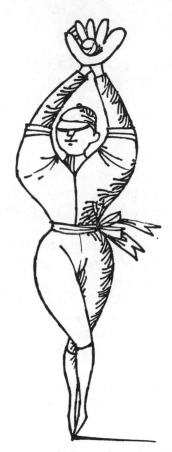

For the most part, my feelings about him I silently conceal,
But when he comments that *The Power of Positive
Thinking* burns with a hard, gemlike flame, I can
only cry that he is robbing Pater to paw Peale.

A MINT OF PHRASES

OR, A TEAM IS AS STRONG AS ITS BENCH

Consider how Time's vasty corridors
Ring with the words of famous orators!
Demosthenes and Billy Graham,
Jeremiah and maybe Nahum,
Patrick Henry and Cicero,
Daniel Webster and Mirabeau,
Burke and William Jennings Bryan,
Pitt the Elder's gifted scion,
The Gracchi, Danton and Disraeli,
Cato fulminating daily,
And other men with names less metric
Who altered history by their rhetoric,
Were their apothegms spontaneous,
Off the cuff, extemporaneous,
Or, soaking in the tub or shaving,
Did they think a thought worth saving,
Roll it on their tongues and smile,
And store it in their future file?
Not even Churchill, without notes,
Could stand and coin such golden quotes
Had he not learned in early days
To hoard each fleeting happy phrase,
And draw on, as he faced the throng,
A bank of jewels five words long.
Eloquence bleeds and weeps and sweats;
Also, eloquence never forgets.

I'M GLAD YOU ASKED THAT QUESTION, BECAUSE IT SHOWS YOU IN YOUR TRUE COLORS

There are times when I despair of my brain;
I can never remember the difference between a heron
    and a crane.
By the collar, I can tell a layman from a cleric,
But I can't tell a crane from a derrick.
To this day, at my brain I am indignant
To think that for years I pronounced "poignant" like a
    backwoods preacher describing the heathen — "po'
    ign'ant."
I do not expect to be sufficiently sibylline
To distinguish a Guelph from a Ghibelline,
But I should know how to tell Cheddar from Stilton, or
    Bel Paese from Camembert,
And I can never rememembert.
I shall now wrap myself in a buffalo robe or sealskin,
And leave all those moot points up to my attorneys,
    Messrs. Rumpel, Rumpel, Mayer & Stiltskin.

HAVE YOU READ ANY GOOD
BOOKS TOMORROW?

Every summer I truly intend
My intellectual sloth to end,
Leave Dumas and Conan Doyle behind me,
And let the dog days, when they find me,
Find me beside the sea perusing
Volumes of Mr. Hutchins' choosing,
Congesting my uncultured head
With famous books I haven't read —
With Milton's *Areopagitica*,
The almanacs of Gotha and Whitaker,
With *Lysistrata* and *The Frogs*,
And lots of Plato's dialogues,
With Darwin's *Voyage of the Beagle*,
Erasmus, and Till Eulenspiegel,
Corneille and Molière and Racine
And *Rasselas* and *The Faerie Queene*.
Every summer with me I wager
That I'll read these masterpieces major.
Each June I make a promise sober,
That I'll be literate by October,
Lose d'Artagnan and Sherlock Holmes
In worthier and weightier tomes,

In Nietzsche and even preachier Germans,
And Donne's more esoteric sermons,
The lofty thought of Abelard,
And Rilke, Kafka, and Kierkegaard;
Loop in one comprehensive lasso
Turgenev, Thomas Aquinas, and Tasso,
The Conquest of Peru, by Prescott,
And *David Harum,* by Edward Westcott.
Of the classics, from *Beowulf* to Baedeker,
I know less than a first or second gradeker,
So every summer I truly intend
My intellectual sloth to end,
And every summer for years and years
I've read *Sherlock Holmes* and *The Three Musketeers.*

DON'T SIT UNDER THE
FAMILY TREE

In every illicit gathering of schoolboys there is one
    sentinel crow,
Who, on the approach of authority, will squawk "Scram!"
    or "Blow!"
In my youth you exclaimed "Cheese it!," a locution no
    longer to be heard even in Rahway,
While in England one hollers, in Latin, "*Cave!*," which
    may be pronounced either "cavy" or "cahway" —
In England, that is, except for Penrith, in Cumberland,
    where the warning cry is one that in my memory
    book I furtively stash;
The sentinel yells "Nash for it!" or, if the danger is
    imminent, simply "Nash!"
This I read in *The Lore and Language of Schoolchildren,*
    by the Opies, Iona and Peter,
And my curiosity couldn't be completer.
What was this shady eponymous ancestor, man or myth?
And what his murky deeds that haunt the tribal memory
    and affright the schoolboys of Penrith?
What crooked course did he steer, carrying what horrid
    cargo,
That his name should have become part of current Cum-
    berland juvenile argot?

It is true that harmless men such as the Earl of Sandwich and General Burnside and the Reverend Mr. Spooner have bequeathed their names to our daily speech,

But I fear that Nash could have given marked cards and spades to each;

I fear he was an unsavory wretch,

That he has weaseled into our common tongue in company with Boycott and Burke, with Quisling and Jack Ketch.

I sink beneath this heritage of shame I never knew I had,

And I think that, until it has blown over, to something less execrable I shall change my name, such as Ogden de Sade.

ALL QUIET ALONG THE POTOMAC, EXCEPT THE LETTER G

The table talk in Washington,
I hear by special messenger,
Is brightened by the presence there
Of Kiplinger and Kissinger.

The anecdoes are wittier,
The chitterchat flows ripplinger,
As of the moment on the bus
When Kissinger met Kiplinger.

"My name is Mr. Kiplinger,"
Said Kiplinger to Kissinger.
"And I'm Professor Kissinger,"
Replied his fellow passenger.

"You'll kindly note my g is hard,"
Said Kiplinger to Kissinger;
"Some people call me Kiplinjer,
And nothing is depressinjer."

"Hard g to me," said Kissinger,
"Is sentimental goo.

Kissing-er means more osculant.
More osculant than who?"

"One dowager," said Kiplinger,
"She goes beyond Kiplinjery.
She dragged me to the opera
To add Yseult to injury."

Kiplinger grew progressively pressinger;
"Do you know my good friend Arthur Schlesinger?"
Kissinger answered his fellow passenger,
"No, but I know an Arthur Schlesinger.
In a city named for George or Martha,
How odd that we each should know an Arthur!
Let's have a foursome at Burning Tree,
Your Arthur and you against mine and me."

PHILOLOGY, ETYMOLOGY, YOU OWE ME AN APOLOGY

The more I grow less young
The more I grow bewildered by my mother tongue.
There are words that bring me up short, subpoena-like,
Because they look different but then turn out to mean
  alike.
If anyone wants proof,
Let me point out one such booby trap, or spoof.
It is familiar to any motorist who, a few years ago, found
    his progress impeded by a crawling truck which
    was unfortunately not rammable
Because its behind bore the ominous word, *Inflammable.*
Today the same motorist finds the same truck still un-
    rammable,
But this time because it is labeled *Flammable.*
I have convened myself in a one-man conventicle
And ascertained that although the appearance of *flam-
    mable* and *inflammable* is indeed opposite, their
    meaning is identical.
Last night after murmuring my Now I lay me
I concluded by analogy that *sane* and *insane* are also
    probably synonymous, and in the world we live in
    who is to gainsay me?

SHALL WE DANCE?

BEING THE CONFESSIONS OF
A BALLETRAMUS

I

I've a private, a personal problem
That I brood upon *in petto:*
What kind of mane is a ballet fan,
Ballayo or balletto?
Ballayomane has an ugly sound,
Ballettomane even uglier.
Does the language contain no apposite noun
That would fit the palate snuglier?
O ballayomanes, or ballettomanes,
I'm a testier man than Job;
I renounce you both, and pronounce myself
A confirmed terpsichorephobe.

II

I learned my French by working hard
At listening to Hildegarde.
That's why a word like *"entrechat"*
Is something *je ne comprends pas.*

Is it a stage direction that
Calls for the advent of a cat?
Assume a comma in the center:
Does *"entre, chat"* bid cat to enter?
Let's start again. Does *"entre"* mean
"Among," or possibly "between"?
I find I cannot swallow that;
How do you get between one cat?
Let's forget the tiresome *entrechat*
And watch a *danse du ventrechat.*

THE STRANGE CASE
OF CLASHING CULTURES

In Buffalo there lived an Anglophile, and the future was
  something he preferred to look away from rather than
  toward.
So he read little but the works of Trollope and Mrs.
  Humphry Ward.
He kept his Briticisms in good order,
Partly for his fellow Americans, but mostly for the
  provincials just across the border.
People learned to stare at him glumly
When he explained the origin of his name, which was
  Chumley.
They always said Yes, we know, it started out as Chol-
  mondely,
But he always proceeded fondly;
Undeterred by their Oh shuckses and Piffles,
He would run the gamut of Anglo-American pronuncia-
  tion jokes from Sevenoaks and Snooks and schedule
  and shoolboy to Niagara Falls and Niffles.
He missed many appointments because he wrote his dates
  9/12 or 2/3 instead of 12/9 or 3/2,
And he was constantly struggling for fuller employment
  of the letter *u*.
He once dictated a letter about his tailor's bill which his
  secretary set down, "On my honor you shall see the
  color of my money," and she gave it to him to peruse,
And he testily told her to re-type it, putting in the *u*'s,

And she took no chances since she knew him to be
  fanatical as well as funny,
So she did retype it, "On my honour youse shall see the
  colour of my money."
He was one whom the fact that the English hundred-
  weight is 112 pounds could not nonplus,
And he dressed for dinner every evening the time he
  crossed the continent by bus.
He followed transatlantic custom with his fork and
  knife,
And once nearly finished a competition in the *New States-
  man* and a crossword puzzle in *Country Life*.
He knew Michaelmas from Lady Day, and he regarded
  the recent creation of lifetime peerages as one of
  the greater sociological catastrophes,
And when he spoke of huntin' and shootin' he pronounced the apostrophes.
His neighbors were tolerant, but finally he aroused their
  dander and their ginger;
He proposed that the name of Buffalo be changed to
  Bison because the true buffalo is only to be found in
  Indja.
A committee of prominent citizens tossed him with one
  toss over both Niagara Falls and Niffles,
An act they later regretted, because without his little
  quirks to discuss their conversation became as bare
  as a whiffle-tree shorn of whiffles.

A STRANGE CASEMENT OF THE POETIC APOTHECARY

Poets are always in search of the right word, the adjective
    that is inevitable,
Because an ill-chosen adjective induces levity in the
    reader, and no poet wishes to be levitable.
A poem filled with the right words is more enjoyable,
    and therefore takes longer to read;
Hence the old Louisiana saying "The *mot juste*, the less
    speed."
When, for instance, Keats refers to "magic" casements he
    is no poetaster who a mass of trite, meaningless
    phrases spawns;
He did not slap down the first adjective that came to mind
    because he had left his thesaurus at Fanny Brawne's.
Whosoever thinks so, his ignorance of both Keats and
    casements is absurd;
If Keats speaks of a casement as "opening," then "magic"
    is the only possible word.
In the matter of casements Keats was no dreamy loto-
    phagic;
He knew that if a casement was either openable or
    shuttable it was manifestly magic.

Keats could have written a lot more odes and died with
money in the bank
But for the long hours he wasted trying to twist little
widgets that were rusted stuck and yanking handles
that wouldn't yank.
If his casements were like mine, when open they would
not admit the breeze, and when shut they would
not exclude the rain,
And when he looked through them he could not see Shelley or anything else plain.
So anybody who thinks there is a *juster mot* than "magic,"
I suggest they join the lowing herd and wind slowly
o'er the lea,
And leave casements to Keats and to me.

YOU'LL DRINK YOUR ORANGE
JUICE AND LIKE IT,
COMRADE

Soviet Union agrees to absorb quantities of citrus fruits
to relieve Cyprus surplus. — *Newspaper item.*

There's a Cyprus citrus surplus,
Citrus surplus Cypriotic.
No Sicilian citrus surplus
But a Cyprus citrus surplus,
Not a Cyprus citron surplus
But a Cyprus citrus surplus,
Not a Cyprus citrus circus
But a Cyprus citrus surplus.
It's a special citrus surplus,
Cyprus citrus super surplus.
"Just a surface citrus surfeit,"
Says a cryptic Coptic skeptic.
But the bishop in his surplice
Certifies the surfeit citrus —
In his surplus Sunday surplice,
Certifies the citrus surfeit.
Who'll assimilate the surplus,
Siphon off the Cyprus citrus?

Sipping at the citrus cistern,
Who'll suppress the Cyprus surplus?
Says the Soviet to Cyprus,
"Send us all your surplus citrus;
This is just a simple sample
Of Socialist assistance.
Should you show a similar surplus
In the simmering summer solstice,
Send a summons to the Soviet
For surplus citrus solace."

Now on Cyprus they're all reading
Victory, by Joseph Comrade.

THE BOOK OF PROVERBS

A WORD TO HUSBANDS

To keep your marriage brimming,
With love in the loving cup,
Whenever you're wrong, admit it;
Whenever you're right, shut up.

800-490-7733